W9-BTI-086

Author:
Jacqueline Morley studied English literature at Oxford University. She has taught English and history and now works as a freelance writer. She has written historical fiction and nonfiction for children.

Artist:
David Antram was born in Brighton, England, in 1958. He studied at Eastbourne College of Art and then worked in advertising for 15 years before becoming a full-time artist. He has illustrated many children's nonfiction books.

Series creator:
David Salariya was born in Dundee, Scotland. He has illustrated a wide range of books and has created and designed many new series for publishers in the UK and overseas. David established The Salariya Book Company in 1989. He lives in Brighton with his wife, illustrator Shirley Willis, and their son, Jonathan.

Editor: Stephen Haynes

Editorial Assistant: Mark Williams

Published in Great Britain in 2013 by
The Salariya Book Company Ltd
25 Marlborough Place, Brighton BN1 1UB

ISBN-13: 978-0-531-25944-3 (lib. bdg.) 978-0-531-23041-1 (pbk.)

Published in 2013 in the United States
by Franklin Watts
An imprint of Scholastic Inc.
Published simultaneously in Canada.

A CIP catalog record for this book is available from the Library of Congress.

Printed and bound in China.
Printed on paper from sustainable sources.
1 2 3 4 5 6 7 8 9 10 R 22 21 20 19 18 17 16 15 14 13

You Wouldn't Want to Meet Typhoid Mary!

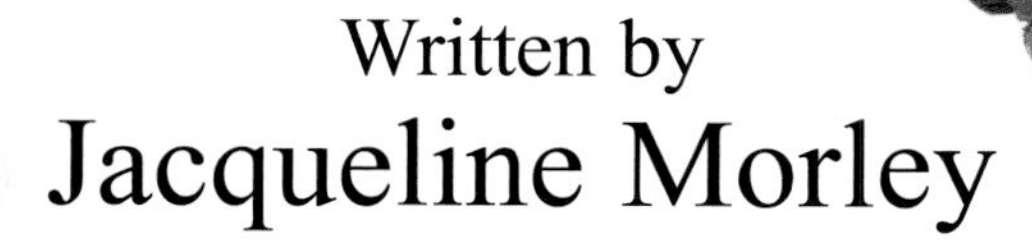

Written by
Jacqueline Morley

Illustrated by
David Antram

Created and designed by
David Salariya

A Deadly Cook You'd Rather Not Know

Franklin Watts®
An Imprint of Scholastic Inc.
NEW YORK • TORONTO • LONDON • AUCKLAND • SYDNEY
MEXICO CITY • NEW DELHI • HONG KONG
DANBURY, CONNECTICUT

Contents

Introduction

It's June 20, 1909. You're a New York journalist flipping through the Sunday papers over breakfast to see what your rivals have to say. In the *New York American* you find a sensational article about a deadly disease.

"TYPHOID MARY"

Extraordinary Trail of Death and Disease

MARY MALLON, an apparently healthy New York cook, has been found to be breeding deadly typhoid fever germs inside her digestive tract. She sheds them wherever she works. The food she dishes up is fatal. Yet Mary denies that she is responsible for the frequent typhoid cases in families where she has worked as a cook. To protect the public, the New York Health Authority is keeping her prisoner in an isolation hospital—perhaps for life—though she is not guilty of any crime and has not broken the law.

Death in the Kitchen!

IF THIS STORY IS TRUE, you certainly wouldn't want to meet "Typhoid Mary"—the thought of it makes you lose your appetite. The paper is calling her the most dangerous woman in America. Yet you can't believe she's really such a monster. This gives you an idea for an article: "Typhoid Mary, the Truth Behind the Headlines." What's the real story behind the woman they call Typhoid Mary?

Typhoid fever is a disease spread by bacteria in water or food. It causes high fever and severe diarrhea. Some victims die of dehydration (loss of water from the body) or other complications.

A Really Good Cook

First you interview city banker Charles Warren. "In 1906," he tells you, "we rented a holiday house on Long Island and hired servants locally. Mary Mallon came to us as cook. She was a good one. Her ice cream, mixed with fresh peaches,* was a winner. She left about three weeks after we got typhoid fever. Happily, none of us died."

You wonder: Did Mary go because she knew she was to blame? But if so, why didn't she leave at once?

**Cooking kills most germs, but raw, unwashed food such as fresh fruit can carry them.*

Mary's Career

MARY won't discuss her past. You know only that she was born in Ireland in 1869 and came to the United States, alone and barely 15 years old, to find work.

SHE HAD NO TRAINING and took various low-paying jobs, until eventually she persuaded an employment agency that she could cook.

SHE'S BEEN COOKING for wealthy New York families for years now, so the Warrens were quite happy to take her on. She seems to be in excellent health.

Fever Strikes

THE FIRST PERSON to fall sick is the Warrens' younger daughter, Margaret. The doctor's diagnosis is typhoid fever.

SOON Margaret's mother, sister, two of the maids, and the gardener show the same symptoms: soaring temperature, low pulse rate, nosebleed, nausea, and diarrhea.

WITH NO TYPHOID FEVER anywhere else on Long Island, the source of infection must be in the house. Experts check the drains but find nothing wrong.

Tracing the Culprit

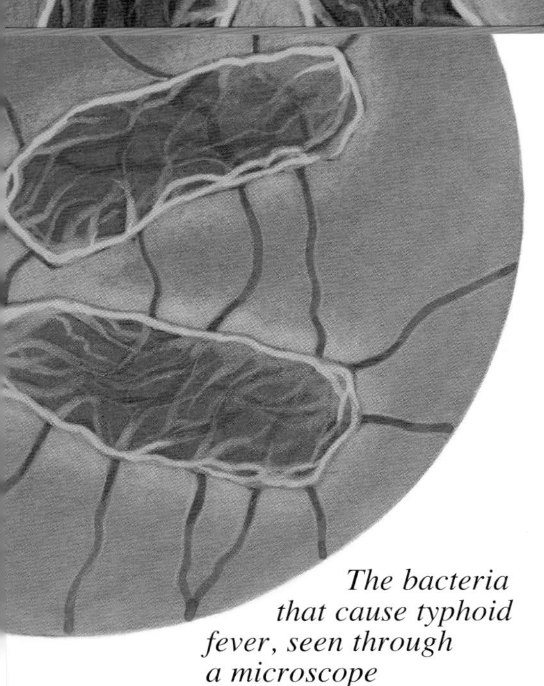

The bacteria that cause typhoid fever, seen through a microscope

Next you visit sanitary engineer George Soper. "The house had been given the all clear," he tells you, "so I checked on the people. Any newcomers at around that time? 'We had a new cook,' the Warrens said. That was the clue! New research shows that some people are 'carriers' of a disease. That means they go on breeding its germs long after they've gotten over the illness. They may not even know they've had it. To see if Mary was a carrier, I traced her job history through employment agency records."

Bacteria: The New Enemy

TYPHOID FEVER is claiming over 35,000 lives a year in the United States at this time. For centuries it was believed that such diseases were caused by "bad air" created by dirty living conditions.

BY THE 1880s, scientists in France and Germany had proved that many diseases, including typhoid fever, are caused by bacteria—tiny living organisms passed from person to person in water and uncooked food.

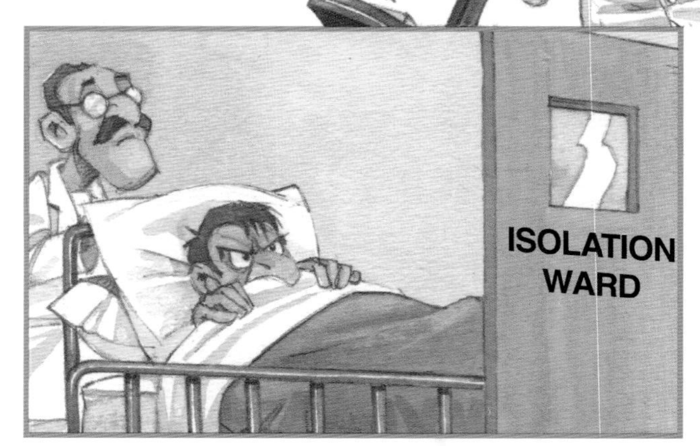

PUBLIC HEALTH AUTHORITIES have been given the power to isolate people with dangerous diseases from people who are healthy—by force if necessary.

Mallon, did you say? It rings a bell, Mr. Soper.
BEST STAFF SUPPLIED
Handy Hint
Keep up with the latest research on how diseases spread. It could save lives.
SOPER FINDS that in the last ten years, typhoid fever occurred in at least seven households in which Mary Mallon was cook.
1. Summer 1900: visitor gets typhoid fever.
2. Winter 1901-1902: laundress catches it.
3. Summer 1902: seven people infected.
4. Summer 1904: four servants infected.
5. Summer 1906: six members of the Warren household fall sick.
6. Fall 1906: laundress ill.
7. Winter 1907: Bowen family—chambermaid sick, daughter of family dies.
8. ?

A Hot Reception

"Before I could report Mary to the authorities," Soper explains, "I needed proof that she was breeding bacteria. I found she was cooking for some people called Bowen, so I called on her with what I thought was a reasonable request. I told her I needed to take samples of her blood, urine, and feces to test them for signs of bacteria. She refused to listen! She seemed to think I was making disgusting suggestions and accusing her of a crime. She flew into a rage and went for me with a carving fork."

You wonder: If Soper had been more tactful, might Mary have listened to what he had to say?

Handy Hint

If your job involves asking awkward questions, be prepared for some awkward answers.

A Home Visit

WITH A COLLEAGUE to back him up, Soper tries again at Mary's lodgings. They have to climb a lot of stairs, and at the top they get a very hostile reception.

THEY LEAVE in a hurry and are followed by violent yelling from the top of the stairs.

A Woman's Touch

“I reported Mary to the New York City Health Authority,” Soper tells you. “The sanitary inspector thought she might listen to a woman, so he sent his assistant, Dr. Sara Josephine Baker, to the Bowens’ house. Mary was totally uncooperative, so Dr. Baker returned the next day with five police officers and an ambulance. Mary was on the lookout with the carving fork. There was a scuffle on the doorstep, and by the time they got in Mary had disappeared.”

Handy Hint

If you know you're not welcome, put your foot in the door when it opens.

After Dr. Baker's failed first attempt to see Mary, her boss gets tough with her.

Anxious to get results, Dr. Baker searches the entire house. The servants are no help. They say they know nothing.

A Scrap of Cloth

"I couldn't believe it," says Dr. Baker when you ask her about that day. "Mary had completely vanished. We spent five hours searching every nook and cranny of the Bowens' house and the house next door. The servants would say nothing. They were obviously taking Mary's side against interfering officials and the police.

"Finally, one of the policemen spotted a tiny scrap of blue calico caught in the door of the closet under the front steps. We hadn't looked inside there before, because there was a whole stack of overflowing trash cans piled against the door. The servants must have stacked them up there once Mary was inside. She came out fighting and yelling. She was very good at both."

FOOTPRINTS IN THE SNOW lead the police to a chair set up near the fence separating the Bowens' property from the property next door. This prompts them to search the next-door house as well.

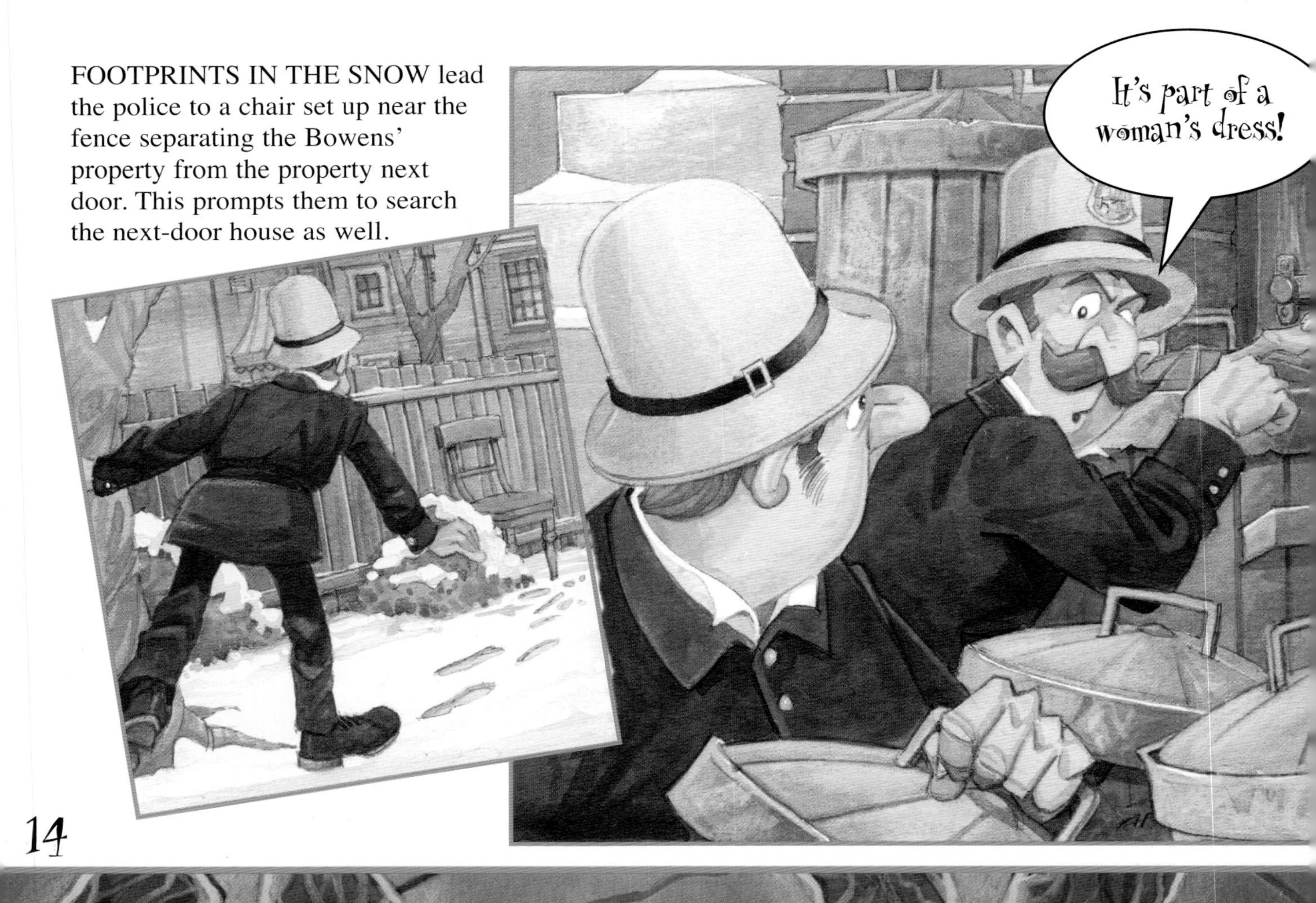

I've done nothing wrong! I've never had typhoid in my life!
Handy Hint
When you've looked for someone in all the possible places, try the impossible ones.
It's like being in a cage with an angry lion.
IT TAKES several policemen to get Mary into the ambulance. Dr. Baker then has to sit on her for the whole ride.

What the Tests Showed

Next you interview the superintendent of Willard Parker Hospital, where Mary was taken. "Tests proved her insides were teeming with bacteria," he tells you. "We tried giving her medicines to stop it, but nothing worked. In fact, we tried so many that she probably thought we didn't know what we were doing.

"When we suggested removing her gallbladder, it was the last straw for her. She wouldn't allow it." You wonder: If they'd concentrated less on zapping bacteria and more on talking things over with her, might she have cooperated?

SOPER TELLS MARY in the hospital that if she answers his questions they can publish a book on her case. He'll write it and she'll get the profits.

WITHOUT A WORD, Mary glares at him, pulls her bathrobe around her, goes into the bathroom, and slams the door in his face.

Handy Hint

If you're asked to agree to something you don't see the point of, it's probably safest to say no.

SPECIAL DIETS, together with laxatives, brewer's yeast, and urotropin (to sterilize urine), are tried on Mary without any success.

MARY IS A GIFT to scientific research. The hospital tests her blood, urine, and feces regularly to study how a carrier's bacteria production varies.

Isolated!

"Mary wouldn't see reason. She insisted she was a healthy woman, had never had typhoid fever, and couldn't possibly pass it on. So what could we do?" the superintendent asks. "We have to protect the public, and with that sort of attitude she was a threat to everyone's health. So we sent her to Riverside Isolation Hospital."

Riverside Hospital is on North Brother Island in New York's East River, opposite the Bronx. Its patients have no way of leaving. Most of them suffer from tuberculosis and hope to leave when they're better, but there is no such hope for Mary. She is housed apart from them in a cabin by the river, with only a fox terrier to keep her company.

FROM HER WINDOW Mary watches the ferry taking lucky patients back to the mainland—and freedom.

MARY IS ALLOWED to be with hospital staff and to help out with chores that do not involve cooking or handling food.

A NURSE hints that Mary might be freed if she promises to go to a sister in Connecticut and never return to New York. That way the New York authorities would be rid of her. But Mary has no sister and refuses to lie.

Handy Hint
If you refuse to do what your doctors say you must do, you can't expect them to let you out.
That's her, the kidnapped woman.*
* Mary actually overheard someone saying this about her.

Habeas Corpus

If the authorities think they can forget about Mary, they are wrong. In 1909 she starts a legal process known as a writ of "habeas corpus."* This is an order saying that a prisoner must be produced in court so that a judge can say whether the imprisonment is lawful.

Mary's case goes to the New York State Supreme Court, and that's why you've just read about her in the newspapers. The judge has accepted the health authority's reasoning and declared Mary's imprisonment lawful. You wonder: The law allows the authorities to detain *sick* persons who endanger the health of others, but Mary is not actually sick. Mary's lawyer did not make that point in court. Would it have made a difference if he had?

***A Latin phrase, originating in medieval English law. It means "You may have the body."**

For and Against

MARY'S LAWYER argues that the health authority acted wrongly. It should have let her appeal to a judge before taking away her liberty.

FOR THE PAST YEAR Mary has been smuggling out her own samples of feces and urine for testing in a private laboratory. The results show no evidence of typhoid fever.

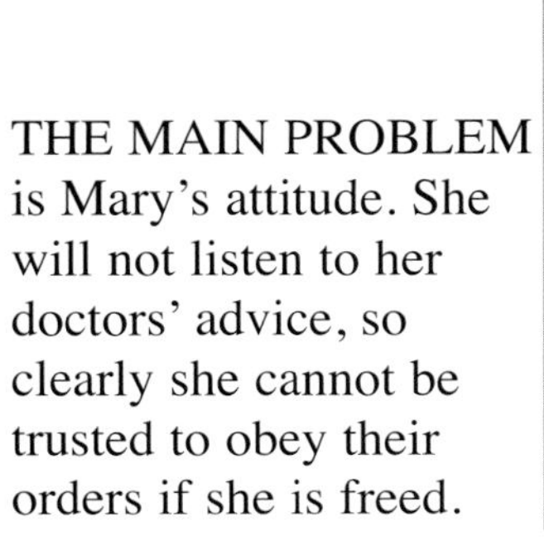

THE MAIN PROBLEM is Mary's attitude. She will not listen to her doctors' advice, so clearly she cannot be trusted to obey their orders if she is freed.

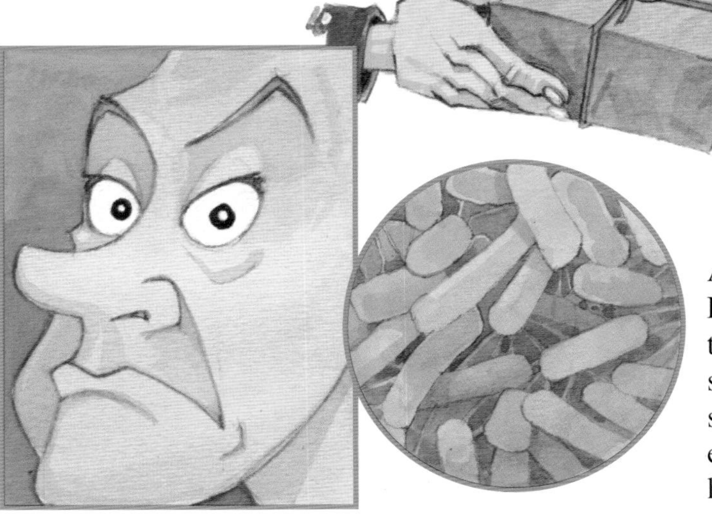

A DOCTOR from the Riverside Hospital testifies that most of Mary's samples swarm with bacteria, but some don't—which explains why some tests have negative results.

ALL THIS PUBLICITY brings Mary a proposal of marriage from a Michigan farmer. She turns him down.

Mary Gets a Break

Mary's hopes collapse. She is sent back to North Brother Island. But in 1910, her luck changes. A new health commissioner is appointed who thinks Mary has been treated harshly. It's known by now that there are thousands of healthy carriers around. They can't all be locked away. Provided they understand what being a carrier means, and do not cook or handle food, they are not a danger to other people. The commissioner believes Mary has learned her lesson and can now be trusted. Before releasing her he makes sure she has a job to go to. He finds her work as a laundress.

BEFORE ALLOWING MARY to leave the Riverside Isolation Hospital, the health commissioner makes her sign a legal document in which she promises that she will never again work as a cook.

THE COMMISSIONER briefs the press: "Can't the poor creature be given an opportunity to make a living and have her past forgotten? She is to blame for nothing."

THE HEALTH DEPARTMENT keeps an eye on Mary at first, but after a while she gives them the slip. At the laundry no one has any idea where she can be found.

"Typhoid Mary" Strikes Again

In 1915 a typhoid outbreak at the Sloane Maternity Hospital in New York affects 25 members of the staff. Two of them die. George Soper and Dr. Baker are called in. They learn that the kitchen staff is calling the cook "Typhoid Mary"—just as a joke, of course. Her name is Mrs. Brown. But in the kitchen Dr. Baker recognizes "Mrs. Brown" at once: It's Mary Mallon.

MEANWHILE, in the superintendent's office, Soper is handed a letter written by "Mrs. Brown." He recognizes Mary's handwriting.

NO SOONER is Mary spotted than she vanishes again. She is traced to the borough of Queens, where a health officer sees a heavily veiled woman carrying a bowl of gelatin to a friend—and recognizes Mary.

A POLICE SQUAD goes to arrest her. No one answers the door, so a sergeant pokes his head through an open upper window. He is met with ferocious barking and backs off fast.

THE SERGEANT comes back with hunks of meat that he tosses into the room. That keeps the dogs busy while the search party creeps past.

THE POLICE go through the house, listening for Mary as she flees from room to room. They finally corner her in the bathroom.

Confined for Life

Mary's use of a false name seems to prove that she knows she shouldn't cook and doesn't care what harm she does. You find it difficult to believe that she's as hard-hearted as that—maybe she's convinced the doctors have gotten it all wrong. But the authorities are taking no more chances. They send her back to North Brother Island once and for all.

In time, Mary comes to terms with life there and makes some friends. She's in her fifties when a new young doctor comes to run the hospital laboratory. Mary gets along well with her and is hired as a lab assistant, a job Mary enjoys.

MARY MAKES A LITTLE MONEY by selling her beadwork handicrafts to people on the island.

IN THE LAB Mary helps with simple medical tests and general cleaning up.

DURING THE 1920s, the authorities start allowing Mary to make day trips to the mainland. She always returns to the island. It has become her home.

Good-bye, Mary

Mary dies on North Brother Island on November 11, 1938, having spent a total of 26 years there. The nine mourners who come to her funeral will not give their names to the press.

You wonder: Was it right to keep her prisoner when thousands of (more cooperative) carriers went free? She wasn't guilty of a crime, only of being pigheaded. The public has to be protected, but Mary had a right to a free life. How far should the human rights of one person be limited for the sake of the rest of us?

That is a question people are still trying to answer today.

IN 1931 Mary is photographed with lab colleague Emma Sherman. Emma says Mary is pleasant to be with, as long as no one mentions typhoid.

LATE IN LIFE, Mary draws strength from her Roman Catholic faith. The church's teachings are a great comfort to her.

ON CHRISTMAS MORNING, 1932, Mary is paralyzed by a stroke. She remains bedridden until her death six years later.

Well, I guess she's finally at peace.
Handy Hint
Remember, there's no such thing as perfect freedom. It's a compromise between what you want and what other people need.
MARY MALLON
NOV.11.1938
JESUS MERCY

Glossary

Bacteria Microscopically small organisms of many types, found almost everywhere. Some types (known as "germs") cause disease, while other bacteria do useful work, such as breaking down waste matter.

Bronx, the The northernmost of the five boroughs into which New York City is divided.

Calico A cheap cotton material used to make clothing.

Carrier A person who shows no symptoms of a disease but harbors its germs and can infect other people.

Digestive tract The series of organs (throat, stomach, intestines) through which food passes in the process of being digested, and waste products are eliminated.

East River A tidal strait that separates Long Island from the boroughs of Manhattan and the Bronx in New York City.

Feces The waste product discharged from the bowels after food is digested; excrement.

Gallbladder A small organ below the liver that helps digest fat.

Habeas corpus A legal action through which a person can be released from unlawful imprisonment. It is regarded as the safeguard of individuals from the tyranny of rulers. It was adopted into the United States Constitution from English law.

Isolation hospital A hospital in which patients suffering from infectious diseases are treated. Special precautions are taken to prevent the spread of disease from one person to another.

Long Island A narrow island about 118 miles (190 km) long, lying close to the U.S. mainland and forming part of the state of New York.

New York American A daily newspaper, published from 1901 to

1937, that concentrated on sensational human-interest stories.

North Brother Island An islet in the East River. In the late 1800s, it was basically uninhabited. This made it an ideal location for Riverside Hospital, built there in 1885 as a place to isolate dangerously infectious patients. The island is now abandoned and closed to the public.

Public health authorities Departments of local government developed during the 19th century to protect and promote people's health.

Queens A borough of New York City, located at the western end of Long Island.

Sanitary engineer An expert who designs and builds toilets, drains, sewage treatment plants, and other facilities to dispose of waste products safely. This helps to reduce the spread of disease.

Specimen A sample of a patient's urine or feces, which can be tested in a laboratory to find out whether the patient is suffering from a particular disease.

Stroke A loss of brain function caused by a sudden interruption in the blood supply to the brain.

Typhoid fever (often called **typhoid** for short) A dangerous and sometimes fatal disease spread by eating or drinking something contaminated with bacteria from an infected person's feces. Today, better sanitation and personal hygiene have reduced cases in developed countries, but typhoid fever is still a serious threat worldwide.

Urotropin A powerful antiseptic drug used to treat urinary infections.

Index